Turning Point

Carolyn Williams

ISBN: 978-1-956884-20-3

Contributing Editor: All services completed by Imprint
Productions, Inc.
Cover Design: All services completed by Imprint
Productions, Inc.
Printed in the United States of America Published by
Imprint Productions, Inc.

First Edition 2023

Contact: info@imprintproductionsinc.com
Visit Us: www.imprintproductionsinc.com

Acknowledgements

I'd like to first honor God, the guiding force in my life. My mother Juanita Williams and my late father Robert Franklin Williams, who raised me. Frankie Thomas, my unwavering best friend, I love you dearly. Women in Transition and Chaplain Anika Jones, thank you for inspiring me. To my four sons - Darrell, Terrell, Javis, and Joshua, we've faced quite a journey. Blessings to my daughters-in-law Reshea and BreAnna.

To my grandchildren - Matthew, Khloe, Ja'kobie, Jansen, Raleigh, Lil Joshua Jr., and baby Jayce, I adore you. Aunt Elizabeth McCall, my late grandparents Robert and Ollie Williams, and marital grandparents Son Adam Roberson and Mattie Smith, I remember you all. To my cousin Walt Lee Smith Savannah, thank you for sharing our family history. To Brunetta Nelson, my coach and friend, I appreciate your support on this challenging journey. I've made it through, and to God be the glory.

Dedication

I dedicate this book to my granddaughters, Khloe Michelle Robbins, and Ryleigh Mae Lee. I wish to see them grow into happy, confident young women. Having experienced unhappiness and lack of love myself, I remind Khloe to be confident and beautiful. I don't want them to suffer as I did, so I show them love and respect, encouraging them to excel. I'm here to support them fully, helping them soar in life. Blessings to my girls.

Table of Contents

Chapter 1: Love and War

I never thought life could be so hard. It seems like loving and being loved is even harder. Love can drain you. I had a heart-to-heart with God, asking why I felt unloved by family, friends, boyfriends, and ex-husbands after three failed marriages. I was tired of pretending to be fine when I was hurting inside. I was so tired of bleeding internally, wounded and walking like nothing was wrong. I was smiling on the outside, but inside the hurt was unbearable.

I decided to give God a call. I remembered His word: "Give your attention to what God is doing right now and don't get worked up about what may or may not happen tomorrow. God will help you deal with whatever hard things come up when the time comes." Matthew 6:34 As a woman, I learned to worry less and pray more.

In 2011, I had no idea what I was about to go through in church and at home. I married an Elder and became a First Lady. We had a beautiful June 1st wedding. I will never forget that day: My late father walked me down the aisle. As we made our way down, he whispered, "Stop being nervous." I wondered how in the world he knew I was nervous. I have always been a Daddy's girl. My dad told me after the wedding, that this would be his last time walking me down the aisle. He had walked me down the aisle in my last two weddings. My dad passed away in 2006. This was the beginning of my hurt.

No man has ever loved me the way my father did. No father wants to see anyone hurt his daughter. Just the thought of my father brings me to tears right now.

The Blind Side of Love

I received the most hurt from a man of the cloth than I received from an unsaved man. I was never married to anyone who hurt me so bad in my life. He took me through affairs, gambling, selling drugs, and drinking. I cried myself to sleep plenty of nights through it all.

I remember being called at work by a family friend and being told that my husband was having oral sex with other women. I was so angry. I called and told him what I'd heard. He was silent, so I assumed that it was true. In my anger, I called him a wide mouth bass and hung up. I loved my husband, and I didn't want to believe what was happening – until my so-called best friend came up pregnant. I was the only one who didn't know what was going on. He told me he was going out of town for business, but never returned home.

We owned a business, Heavenly Treasures Boutique, which he took credit for starting. It was a vision God gave me and it was taken over by my spouse. It went from selling church clothing to urban wear. The Lord never told me to sell anything other than church clothing. When he left me, he took all my clothing and hid at his family's house. He had everyone thinking he started the business, and that all the money was his.

On top of the infidelity and theft, he was selling drugs, drinking, and gambling. People called him "the dirty preacher," because he was rumored to be doing cocaine. There were countless moments of pain. My youngest son would come into my room in the morning and ask, "Where is your husband? He didn't come home last night." These moments hurt the most because my sons were watching all the mistreatment. He never showed any respect for himself or my kids at that time or even towards me. I so wanted my marriage to work out, but there wasn't much success.

I remember my mother-in-law telling me that I work too much. But I knew if I didn't work, bills would not be paid. I spent ten years with this man, and he never paid any of the bills. I worked two jobs to take care of myself and my kids. There were times he would take his son out to eat and leave me and my boys in the house with no food. My stepson would come back and tell me his dad had plenty of money. He just told *me* he didn't have any. He worked every day as a truck driver and would tell me at the end of the week that he had no money.

The Shift

I noticed out of all the people in his life, he acted as if he hated me with a passion. One day, an older lady told me, "Honey, your husband is your greatest enemy." I was at a loss for words – I couldn't respond. I remember going to do laundry, and an older woman whose husband was a Bishop in the community was there doing laundry too. We talked and I told her about a dream I had the night before. In the dream, I heard God say I was married to a backslider. I didn't understand what the dream meant, but she did. She asked me if I was having marital problems. I immediately became angry. I told her no, but they were on their way or already happening and I couldn't see it.

Men who hurt women are hurt individuals themselves. I was mishandled, disrespected, and unprotected by the man that was supposed to love me. Someone who was supposed to love me as Christ loves the church. It really hurt. I felt like my energy to love him was used to destroy me. I was always trying, but who was trying for me? Always fighting, but who was fighting for me? In all that I have been through, I believe I have a right to be loved. I deserve to be loved *correctly*.

I have cried myself to sleep many nights asking the Lord, "Why me? What did I do wrong?" I remember when I was very young, twenty-six to be exact. My youngest son's father told me after I had given birth to his son that he never loved me, he only told me what I wanted to hear. He left me for another woman two weeks after I had given birth. He said after me, he was going to get him a "fly ass bitch." So, what was he saying to me? It sounds like I wasn't anything to him.

Clarity

In 2013, my whole life changed. I was divorced, had been through three relationships, and none of them were successful. I was at the point of not caring about anything. I was bitter, hurt, confused, and angry with everyone. I shed many tears at the end of that relationship. I felt an unbelievable amount of hurt after ten years. I remember sending my mother a photo as "the new me." My mother told me she didn't recognize me. She said she wanted to send him a thank you note for leaving me. You would never believe someone could make you *look* so awful.

Sometimes, when you see what you want, you forget what you need. What you accept is far from what you deserve. Don't let the pain of any past relationship prevent you from finding something genuine and real in the future.

From Chris and our divorce, I dated three men in our hometown. They all knew I was a very good woman, and they all knew Chris somehow. One was a high school sweetheart. I remember him saying, "You let Chris do this and that…" The first thing that came to my mind was that

Chris was my husband. The man I was dating thought he could use me. It makes me angry just thinking about it.

Nobody was there like my Aunt Liz. She worried about me day and night. I would call her and my pastor friend daily. These two ladies showed compassion in my time of trouble. In a time where it seemed like I was hurt so much that I wanted to hurt back. They say hurt people, hurt people.

Chapter 2: In the Hills

I was a beautiful broken young woman! I believe I was absent from myself, as strange as that may seem. I remember my father telling me that that would be his last time walking me down the aisle. My ex-husband said, "Oh! Don't worry about that!" From that moment until the end of our marriage, I suffered from a broken heart. I repeatedly met the same types of men one after the other. I would ask myself what's wrong with me? Why does no one want to love me? I would even ask some of the men, until I heard God say, "There is *NOTHING* wrong with you!"

On Saturday, March 13, 2021, I watched my second oldest child get married. I was so proud of my son. I had a dance with him, and we just talked and talked. He said, "Momma, I am gonna be a good husband, I promise I got this!" I believed him. My sons know I always told them not to treat any woman the way you saw me treated.

I also told him, "I am your mother, I know this. I will always love you, but your wife comes first, even before me." This was understood even before he said, "I do." I knew how it was. I had a mother-in-law who thought her son did no wrong. I believe in God's way. I cried as my daughter-in-law came down the aisle. I saw my son break down and cry. She was so astonishing in her beauty!

I told my pastor that Sunday, "Well I got two sons down and two to go, and myself!" We both laughed. Yet, seriously, I would love to be married again to a God-fearing, good man.

Blessings and Lessons

As the pastor said on Sunday, everything is going down, but the word of God. I truly believe this in my heart. I have suffered much at the hands of men. The Bible clearly says not to put your trust in man and every time I got married and fell in love in a relationship, I put my trust in man. My family and friends all saw that when I was in a relationship, I loved hard.

I remember back in Screven County 2013; I had been dating a guy for two years. He promised to marry me, but he didn't. Instead, he quit his job of nine years and stayed with me. A year later he found someone in Hampton, South Carolina, got a job and left me. The woman would call me and tell me to stop calling his phone and let me know they'd been together for x amount of months. Now here it was I was paying the bill, so I had the phone turned off. I treated him just as good as others, yet I had not had any man in my life to love me wholeheartedly.

My twin sister used to tell me, "When you get rid of a no-good man, you feel better about yourself. You won't be asking yourself, 'What's wrong with you?' You'll say, "I am a wonderful woman, a good woman, and God said everything He created was good. That includes me!" My twin sister should know how good it feels to let someone go. There was a time when a guy lived with my sister. Along came a woman who was supposed to be his sister, but later we found out it was his girlfriend. My sister was hurt and angry and she had every right to be mad. The nerve of that guy! Men really do some nasty things to women. We as women should not allow our dignity to be taken.

I have a very good friend, older than me, she's a very encouraging woman. I love her a lot. She teaches me how to be a good woman and how to carry myself. I love her spirit. Years ago, after I left my ex-husband, I came to Atlanta, GA and when I came, I was a hurt individual trying to rebuild my life. I had an empty apartment. I'd sit on the floor with nothing inside. I only had $1500 dollars in my pocket. As I sat there on the floor, the Chaplin I met here called me. She asked if I was home and I said yes. The next thing I know, they were there with a U-Haul truck and two cars. The Chaplin had rounded up a few people and came with things to fill every room in my apartment. I just asked my God "what next?" and he showed me that very second.

Overcoming Obstacles

I had just gotten out of the halfway house. I spent two and a half years behind prison walls for taking money from my job. I committed this crime after my divorce when I was sad, hurt, and desperate. It seemed like no one cared for me. I had family hurt and no real relationship with my children and the man I had married had unjustly left me for my so-called best friend, who by the way told me she was never my friend. I now believe she was not. I noticed that I love hard and when I stop loving, there is nothing anyone can say or do. You never feel the same any longer.

This experience could have caused me to lose my mind. I remember a conversation with a lady who told me that someone had said something so terrible to her that if she didn't have a strong mind, she might have gone off and killed herself. Regardless of our skin color, as a human race, we must learn how to treat each other.

There were a lot of dysfunctions in my family, a fact that some may dispute. Although I have vivid memories, when I bring them up, I'm called a liar. Most people want to avoid speaking on family matters, but some people feel a breath of fresh air talking about our past. Personally, I feel suffocated—I can't confide in my family because they wouldn't understand me. A Chaplain once asked me why I consistently felt unloved. My answer: I felt like my mother loved all my siblings more than she loved me. I know she loved me because I was her child, yet I felt like she put all my siblings before me. I never felt like our bond was strong like the bond she had with my sisters. I felt like I had to pay for everyone's love.

My need to please everyone else became a habit throughout my life, but the people I was trying to please and provide for showed little reciprocation. Have you ever felt profound loneliness? I mean the kind of loneliness that makes you feel like you can't talk to anyone about the troubles in your mind. That's how I felt!

I learned a long time ago that Jesus Christ listens to me. I talk to him often. I asked him, "Why do bad things happen to good people?" I began to see my life shifting as I grew older. I had to make changes to better myself, so I stepped back and listed the steps I would take:

1. Slow all the way down
2. Invest time into myself
3. Remove people from my life so I can grow

When I did these three things, I felt better about myself. I could smile and laugh and feel good about it.

Chapter 3: Understanding Me

When I would try to get into a relationship, I would always leave out the hurt parts of myself. As I said earlier, I think I love so hard and so sincerely that people take me for granted. Everybody wants someone to love them. Today, as I'm writing this book, I take pride in myself as a woman. I know how to adjust to being alone and trust me – it feels good! I'm not saying I don't get lonely, but I am learning how to be alone.

There are many times I thought I was in romantic relationships, but they failed. I had three failed marriages. I believe I was only in love with the third husband. My first husband was just too young to understand love. I thought there was something to gain with the second husband; I wanted to live well and I thought he had money which was an awful reason to marry. I really wanted my marriage to my third husband to work. I really loved this man, even when my family hated the ground he walked on.

This was the marriage that really broke me. I lost so much weight. I stopped going to church for a year and I kept asking God, "How could you allow this?" Maybe a year later, I realized pain comes with a purpose. I was embarrassed that he left me for nothing. I considered myself a good wife. I went to church, work, and came home. Now I see we never did anything together. I worked two jobs and that was only because he wouldn't pay any bills for our home the way he should have.

I am sharing my story, so people don't make the same mistakes I did. They say love doesn't hurt, but I beg to differ. I was feeling love, hate, retaliation, resentment, and unforgiveness. The reflection of it all made me more aware of myself. The reflection of all these feelings made me more aware of myself.

My Walk with the Lord

The Lord is so good to me, and I had to repent and forgive. I have been in a lot of relationships with family, friends, associates, and lovers – married and unmarried. I thank God for delivering so many things. We are all "ex" something or ex-ed out of somethings. I forgave my ex-husband, but I had a hard time forgiving his baby's mother. I now ask myself why I was angrier at her than him, when they were both wrong. I must work on removing that from the heart where she is concerned, so I openly admit my feelings about her.

My ex-husband was not my only hurt. I moved to Atlanta, GA to get away from all my pain. It took me a long time to love someone else. I met a gentleman from New Jersey, and I thought he was very attractive and friendly. Somewhere deep within him, I saw a hurt man. I made the wrong choice trying to be the person to show him love and affection. I should have run as fast as I could, but I stayed for six years. He never showed any respect for me. He always cursed and belittled me in front of all his family and so-called friends. When I kept his nieces, he would even tell them to disrespect me in my own house.

I was tired of coming home from work and all his friends and family were in my home. He didn't respect me enough to ask them to leave so that I could relax. He would drink and smoke weed all day long. He was even rumored to be on pills and cocaine, and I think that's the truth.

A Mile in My Shoes

What was wrong with me? Yes, I was an older woman, and he knew this the day that we met, and he had no problem with it. In the last few years, I became the old "B" word. That was inexcusable, it made me sad and very angry, and I didn't want to be with anyone who called me those types of names. I asked God every day to move the anger out of me because I know I'm not completely healed, and I need Him to help me daily.

The first week before Mother's Day, I was assaulted by Mr. as I will call him. He was not himself; He cursed at me and threw up gang signs at me and his nephew while his friends watched. He approached me on the front patio, face-to-face and pushed me so hard into the glass door. It made me so angry that I pushed him back and he told me I push like an old lady. Then, he turned around and punched me in my jaw and knocked me unconscious. I don't know how long I was out. When I came to, he spit in my face and said, "Die b****!"

I could see what was going on, but I couldn't move at all. Everyone standing around claimed they didn't see what happened, even though they obviously did. Everyone was saying the same thing – I broke my jaw. But what judge was going to believe that in the state of Georgia?

They claimed they didn't see him hit me, but there was blood on both of our clothing. He cleaned up most of the blood on my front porch and just like a television crime scene, there were some stains overlooked. I'm still trying to understand who does these types of things to women they claim to love. He even called me in the hospital as if I were stupid, telling me I was drunk and did it to myself, when I don't drink or do drugs. We must be careful who we allow into our lives. He was such a mean man. If I would say, "Jesus," he would say, "You and Jesus can kiss my a**." He would get extremely angry if I talked about God or go to church. I had to be a hypocrite because I was living with a man, I was shacking up. How could I be a woman of God with a man in my house? Now, I can serve God and praise Him. I can play my church music and pray without someone cursing and yelling at me.

I had to have a defibrillator in my chest in 2020. All the stress and fear of this man. He once slapped me so hard in my face, then ran into the kitchen and jumped on top of me. When he got up, I laid there wondering what just happened. I thought, "Jesus, I know I did not deserve all the mistreatment." I had a man in my house telling me we don't go together, and he wasn't my man. Yet, I am not dating or seeing anyone else; I can't bring anyone over because he is in my home. It was sad but true, the enemy took over my home. When I came home from work, every one of his family members and friends would be here and act as if I wasn't the woman of the house – there was no respect for my presence.

Chapter 4: Growing Pains

If I did not stay in the house of the Lord, surely, I would have died at his hands. Just the other day, my sister Regina said to me, "I knew he had done other things to you before he broke your jaw." That was the truth, but for so long I hid everything from my family, everyone but my twin sister. When I told her things about the relationship, she told him everything I said, and he beat me even more after that conversation. She told him my family didn't deal with me and my children didn't mess with me. My own family talked about me to this man and my twin sister didn't trust me when I told her I was being abused.

I love my sisters and I don't want to see them hurt but I have suffered a lot of pain from family, friends, husbands, I have had three in this lifetime. I have cried so many times that I am tired, literally, just tired. God has sustained me, so I must stay close to Him. He is my help and without him, I can do nothing.

I feel good when I have good people around me who understand my struggles. People like Chaplain Jones, my good friend Frankie, and Evangelist S. Lanier. These three women have been in my corner in all of what I go through. I have always wanted love and for some reason, I felt I have never gotten what I deserve. I never felt like my mother loved me like my sisters. So that's how this love thing has followed me down the years. It's awful because all I want is to be loved and I can't seem to find it but in ministry. When I open my mouth and my heart on Sunday morning, I get to really participate. I have a great Pastor and First Lady. I love them dearly. I know God wants to use me! A Charge I have and a God to Glorify!

Friends

I met Mr. Roosevelt Trimble during all I've been through, an amazing man, a man that has such a good heart but also has problems. He doesn't tell you his problems and he tries to be strong all the time. I loved this man and I still do even if we'll never be together. We both have so many things going on in our lives, but he encourages me by telling me, "Go back to God. I want to see you do good." He has always told me that, and I want to thank him for that. I won't be the woman to give up on him and I have my reasons. He is sweet but trying at times. He wonders and I think it has a lot to do with his past. It's funny, I can't sleep right now because something is on my mind, so I write. Oh! How I wish to have a peaceful life without error, is that possible?

Last night was not so good, I try not to depend on

medication to sleep, but I found myself deciding which pill tonight. I started praying, asking God to give me rest and a peace of mind. Of course, my prayers were answered immediately. I feel myself growing each day. I also find myself needing to step away from certain people. This too shall pass, in the name of Jesus! I found myself out tonight at the car wash and as they were cleaning the car, I went to the ladies room of course God did his thing. I learned from Pastor Foster who is a great Pastor, he told me when studying the Word to look at small words, they play an important part in your studying.

So tonight, as I stood in front of the paper towel dispenser it said wave your hand and the paper towel will come down, then it said motion activated. Don't you know if you praise God by waving your hands that God through his son Jesus will be motion activated and you can receive in faith that thing which you desire of the Lord. We must learn how to praise God more and worship in spirit and truth.

Reflection

My life has not been easy, God never said it would be. I went through countless relationships, but I know whom I should have been seeking in the first place. I have a very good friend I would like to say, he's been around for some years, there's just no pull for a relationship right now. I know he loves me, and I love him, I don't want anything right now but more Jesus. Roosevelt, is a wonderful loving caring man, will do anything for me but right now we just relaxed knowing we have a great friendship. I admire the man that he is, this is what friendship is about totally.

We have dated for more than three years. He's sweet, and always willing to help me if he can. Yet, something just doesn't go well with me, he's always busy and has no time to spend with me. If I call what you want, I am handling my business. We stopped eating out, going to the movies, even making love occasionally. I used to spend nights with him now I couldn't come over and it was just total disrespect on his part. I hurt from this so bad that my inner person was being sucked out of me and I had forgotten my worth. I must tell my story. I feel like some people will not like it, family, or friends but I must get delivered from my own self hurt. I hurt myself, not the devil. I caused my own hurt, as LeAndria sings 'God Deliver Me'', with Donald Lawrence.

I left my first love which is my God, and my focus was on an individual who did not want me. The relationship was just as bad as the last. The chaplain asked me why? I didn't have an answer. It can't be the person it has to be me because I keep connecting to the same type of men. Men that need me for help and not for the sake of loving the person who I am, so therefore the problem must be me. Then I asked myself the question, do I love myself? Hum! Good question!

I thought I did, so why am I not doing much better? I noticed that a lot of things fall back on coming up as a child. It matters how a child is raised to succeed or fail. I am a parent, and I played a very important part in my son's life. I have four boys. My oldest son I never hear from, my second son lives in the same city I do and does not even visit me. My youngest two who grew up in the house with me are the only two who interact with me. My third oldest used to be very disrespectful, all of them have spoken harshly to me at some point. I often ask myself if I'm that bad of a mother. I have even asked them, but no one has ever given me an answer.

My twin sister and I are on good terms, we often talk about what we went through, our other sister doesn't seem to remember anything. My baby sister was too young to remember. My two younger sisters are very strong and are not considered weak, but I know everybody has their secret moments. I think that even my twin sister is strong, all we have endured but we have both dealt with harsh relationships in our lifetime. I still thank God for this last relationship. It had its ups and downs, but God's Word says to give thanks in all things. I wanted to write about my life because I wanted younger women to excel and be able not to depend on men.

I know everybody wants somebody, but God is first

and foremost. I feel alone but God says I am never alone. I feel alone but God says I am never alone. One thing for sure: you can't play with the enemy and love God at the same time. God is a jealous God! My friend always told me, and she knew I always wanted a relationship that worked, but she said; you don't have to have a man. She knew the countless times I had been hurt. Again, I say it's my own fault!

I don't blame anyone but myself, it's ok, the enemy thought I was gonna lose my mind, I thought I would, but when Roo dumped me all I had was God and God reminded me that I took my eyes off him and laid them all on Roo. Roo in turn reached Pharaoh's heart towards me and I was dumb founded. As I was reading the Word of God March 27th, 2022, I came across the passage of scripture in Romans 8:5-6. It reads as this, for those who are according to the flesh set their minds on the things of the flesh, but those who are according to the spirit, the things of the spirit. For the mind set on the flesh is death, but the mind set on the spirit is life and peace.

According to this passage, because I was in love with a man in the flesh, I was already dead. I love what he did for me, and I loved him in his flesh and my heart was sore for him. This man never really loved me and as I look back, he was very attracted to white females. Why he came into my life is unassured to me still to this day. I do know after he belittled me in front of this woman after 3 yrs. of courtship, it hurt. Spit in my face told me he did not want me and punched me in my face, after pushing me down to the ground. I went out and bought a car in my name and was making the payments, I found another woman in the car with him. I could never drive until I repossessed it on the night I caught him and the female. Oh! Yes, I have to get this out so I can be delivered. Some may be sitting saying you were the dummy, or you were stupid.

Relief

I say, this could be your daughter, sister, niece, aunt, mother, or your friend. By the grace of God, I am free! If nobody ever loves me again, my biological father and my father in Heaven loves me. You better say, Amen! Oh! Praise God! I felt that in Jesus Name! This is not just for me, it's for women like me, it's for my sisters, it's for my niece, it's for my aunties and friends. Come on clap for Jesus being the centerpiece of your joy. Restoration can happen as long as you focus on God almighty. Jesus never complained about anything that happened in his life. By God's grace endured all the way to the cross. I would be a liar if I told you I don't want human love from a man. I desire to be loved, without all the hurt and mistreatment that those men of my past gave. I am a whole woman and I want to be treated like one. I think God that when writing this testimony, I asked a question and my cousin who will not call her name, sent me a Word; she said you teach people how to treat you; it hit me, and I asked myself, did I? My Chaplin also said to me, "Why do you keep running into the same men?" It's you, not them, so if it is me, why do I choose the same path all the time. God help me! God knows I don't understand a lot of my history, but I do know that God has never left me alone even when I felt so all alone.

I began to look at Rachael and Leah and how one was pretty, and one had delicate eyes so, Jacob loved Racheal more, so much more that he worked fourteen years. Wow! I looked at myself, a wife, a mother, working, owning a boutique and my own husband whom I loved did not want me and seemed as if after our marriage no one else did either. There were family and friends who stood back and watched me hurt, some even enjoyed watching the pain and misfortune I went through.

Through it all I made it. I always wanted someone like my father, who I thought was a good man, I did not know anything other until I was in high school that my own father an adultery, I watched my mother hurt and I am telling you she loved my father so much and his infidelity shattered her to the point of not caring. I watched my mother sit on the front row at my father's funeral with no emotion. I also watched my aunt do the same. I remember my aunt telling my mother, I will be there for my children, but I can't cry. She said he made everyone else happy but not me. Lord, can a person really make you heartless until you'd rather see them dead than alive?

Chapter 5: Conversations

God recently took me on a nostalgic journey through movies like "Snapped" and "Fatal Attraction," serving up a stark reminder of the importance of treating people right. It's like He handed me a script from the Bible, chock-full of instructions on the art of righteous living. Now, I'm no saint—I'll admit to possibly doing or saying things that might've caused a sting to someone else. If that's the case, I'm counting on God for a deep cleanse, inside out. I'm feeling a bit like Paul from the Bible; despite life throwing him some serious curveballs, he soldiered on for the sake of the Gospel. I'm adopting that mindset, continuing on this journey for the gospel of truth. Despite the twists and turns, I'll keep praising God, whether for the highs or the lows.

Switching gears to today, I had a heart-to-heart with my youngest son, delving into uncharted territory—things we've never shared or talked about before. As a mother, it was liberating to lay bare my feelings and witness how it resonated with him. Jay, my youngest, is a gem of a child with a beautiful family. I swelled with pride when he tied the knot because he had always declared that he wouldn't let another man raise his children. His perspective on his wife is downright admirable—he firmly believes that even if their paths diverge, she will wholeheartedly care for their kids. Now, that's the kind of admiration every woman deserves.

Alright, let me spill the beans on a wild chapter in my life – 2013, the year I found myself waltzing in and out of court, practically becoming a regular. It felt like a never-ending legal tango that went on for over a year. But here's the kicker – God decided to set up shop right there in the courtroom with me. Every court session, I'd be the last one lingering, with the judge casually suggesting slotting me into the next calendar. Then came March 12, 2014 – D-day, the day I got sentenced.

Now, picture this: I'm standing at the back with a bunch of other ladies awaiting their fate. As we nervously chatted away, guess what? I discover I have a cousin, a complete stranger till that day, going through the same legal circus. Talk about a plot twist! This was my initiation into a whole new world, and turns out, my cousin had some clout in the joint. She vouched for me, and suddenly, I'm flooded with socks, tees, the whole shebang – all based on her word. Call it divine intervention or just a stroke of luck, but these women behind bars were more caring than some folks I'd met on the streets.

Fast forward to a surreal scene behind a cold, uninviting window that weekend – my mother, sister, and kids paying me a visit. I had a meltdown, and there's my mother, the pillar of strength, telling me to hold my head up. Even my oldest son swung by to sprinkle some encouragement. Oh, and here's a twist to the plot – my second oldest son was also doing time on drug charges. Mom cracked a joke about the unlikely scenario of mother and son doing time simultaneously. It stung, but hey, we've got thick skin.

The silver lining? My son, the one behind bars, is now here in Atlanta, Georgia, all grown up and hitched to his college sweetheart. Yep, my seeds (my sons) and I have weathered storms that'd make most heads spin. Not everyone gets it, and those who hear my story might struggle to believe it, but that's the real deal.

God Speaks

Mark 11:24 says: Therefore, I say unto you, What things soever ye desire when you pray, believe that ye receive them, and ye shall have them.

I took a leap of faith and, believe me, it paid off! God is like a full-time miracle worker, always on the clock. Every night, as I cozy up for some shut eye, I make it a point to focus my prayers on what I want and need from the big guy upstairs. And guess what? He's never let me down. Now, I'm rocking a happiness level that's off the charts because I've got my eyes on the prize – life, health, and strength. There was a time when I was this bitter soul, running on empty, desperately craving love from someone. Problem was, there was no human in sight to sprinkle a bit of that magical love dust on me.

Then, out of the blue, a friend dropped some truth bombs on me. "Carolyn, don't you ever think no other woman is better than you!" she declared. And if that wasn't enough, Frankie, the voice of reason, chimed in with, "Don't let nobody put you down, not a soul. Fall in love until you're practically stupid." I was dating her nephew at the time, and she made it crystal clear that our relationship wasn't hanging on him. Her and her husband had always been kind to me, and that nugget of wisdom she tossed my way stuck. Grabbing onto God and refusing to let go was the smartest move I ever made. I'd learned my lesson in prison – no looking back, no doing things that could drag me back into the mess I'd escaped. I'm head over heels for God, but let's be real, life throws challenges that make us blurt out our intentions to turn a new leaf. The tricky part? We sometimes slip back into old habits without even realizing it.

Meanwhile, Satan's just chilling, looking at us and having a good laugh. I've found myself doing things and saying things I swore I wouldn't, feeling like a bit of a fool. But here's the beauty – God's always there, ready to welcome us back with open arms. Oh, how I love Jesus!

Taking a stroll down memory lane, I revisited my childhood, a time when Grandma Ollie and Grandpa were my rock. Their relationship was like a masterclass in love – never a negative vibe, never a foul word tossed around. Grandpa, a provider, and family man also wore the hat of a church deacon, a darn good one at that. Come Saturday, you'd find him cleaning the church, and on Sundays, he was front and center. And get this, he'd slip us a nickel for the offering plate, even when we thought we were all grown up. Those were the days.

Ah, these moments just light up my face! Back in the day, we weren't rolling in riches, but we had something better – each other. It's funny how, as God sprinkled blessings on our family, some folks started acting like they were the ones with a magic wand, forgetting who the real blesser was. Lord, I thank you when I've got a full plate and when I'm scraping the bottom.

I can't help but chuckle at the memories of heading to my grandparents' place and making do with a foot tub bath by a wood heater. It might not have been glamorous, but we were downright happy. Christmas at our house wasn't about fancy PlayStations or designer clothes. Nope, what we had was this invisible suit of love that wrapped us all up, and nobody went to bed hungry. I grew up dreaming of a good life – a marriage, a cozy home in the country, and a stand-up guy for a husband, just like what I thought my dad was. Turns out, he had his own set of issues, running around on my mom, and some of his sisters were practically cheerleaders for his extracurricular activities.

And here's the twist – why do us women sometimes go down that road, knowing darn well how much it stings to be on the receiving end? Guilty as charged – been there, done that, with another woman's husband. It was a mess, and I'm so grateful to say that God pulled me out of that chaos. I could've been hurt, but man, did God keep me in check when I was a hot mess. Then karma decided to pay me a visit, and someone started pulling the same stunt with my boyfriend and husband. Lord, help me deliver some common sense to these folks! The Bible wasn't kidding when it said that warnings come before the whole ship sinks.

Conversations with Myself

Just before I landed in Atlanta, there was this boyfriend hanging in the background before my prison stint. Oddly, his mom wasn't exactly my biggest fan, and she had a knack for tossing negativity my way. To make matters interesting, she decided to set up camp in the house I was paying the bills for. Painful, right? But I had to reclaim my space, so I showed them the door. Fast forward to one fateful Sunday when he was away for the entire weekend, only to call me up, asking to swing by for work. He showed up, headed straight for the shower, and, feeling generous, I let him. But as I stepped in for my turn, a hunch told me to check the laundry. Lo and behold, I discovered a little surprise in his underwear – some kind of serum. All I could muster was a "you nasty" before we called it quits. The dude then jetted off to South Carolina with this other woman, only to ditch her and marry someone else. Real eye-opener, I'm telling you. My boys, bless their hearts, only know half of my story – what they saw and heard during our time together. Some things, I've decided to keep under wraps.

Now, here's where it gets real. My youngest almost turned that guy into a human puzzle, landing himself in Savannah hospital. When I asked him about it, all he could think about was what was in his pocket. Talk about a wake-up call. My son could've been behind bars but thank the heavens for another chance at life. Hallelujah!

Ever wonder why us women tend to bend over backward to make someone else's life better when our own happiness takes a back seat? I woke up with this notion buzzing in my head. It hit me that I've given so much of myself to people who didn't value me. Time to change that narrative.

I've been in the game, buying cars I couldn't even ride in, handing out cash to folks claiming to be broke, only to find out they were splurging my hard-earned money on other women. Talk about feeling despised and rejected; it cut deep, ya know? I was fed lies and treated like yesterday's news. But hey, I straightened my crown because there was nothing wrong with me. I was just getting taken advantage of, and let me tell you, it was a real heartbreaker. If you haven't been through something like this, it's hard to grasp the gravity of it. No pity party, though – I had to swiftly remind myself who I am. Worthy. Time to restore this queen.

Now, let me spill the tea on the very last relationship. I thought he was the bee's knees, but little did I know he had a thing for white women, and I was nowhere close to fitting that bill. The guy strung me along, playing on the fact that I loved him enough to do just about anything. He kept insisting that I was the only one seeing his cash flow while he was

41

supposedly taking care of others. But here's the deal, us women, we're not fools. We can sense when our man is headed north while trying to convince us he's headed south. I remember this lady saying that on the day her daughter was being laid to rest, the dude she was dating went off and married someone else. Men, I tell ya, juggling three ladies at once and we're clueless about each other. Yet, because I kept my relationship grounded in Christ Jesus (plus, no hanky-panky going on), I sensed something fishy. Especially when I stumbled upon those sex enhancement pills in his car. I didn't quite get the whole picture, Roo, until his Aunt gave me a call this morning. She was in tears, recounting how he treated her horribly over the phone, promising to bring her some stuff and then leaving her high and dry. Hearing her cry got me hurting, man. Goes to show, you can be riding high today and hitting rock bottom tomorrow. Life's a rollercoaster, ain't it?

Chapter 6: Advice

Ladies, let me drop some wisdom – straighten your crown, queen. I remember pouring my heart out to Frankie after breaking up with Roo, feeling like he'd stripped away my dignity as a woman. It was time to throw on my queen attire and share the story of how I pulled through. Frankie and her hubby were there, telling me to stop letting anyone treat me like that, but love, deep love, can make you blind to the obvious. I had this hope he'd come around, but the hate in his eyes when he saw me said otherwise. It's a sad truth - when another woman's in the picture, guys suddenly can't stand you. This man pushed me down, spat in my face, punched me, all because he got caught with someone else. I felt so low, degraded by someone I thought had my back from all angles.

I just wanted deliverance; you know? Sometimes, where you're headed, you've got to leave some baggage behind – kids, loved ones, even those closest to you. So, I focused on my book and Christian studies, trying to fill the loneliness with gym sessions, movies, and other distractions. But my absolute favorite day is Sunday – a trip to the House of Worship. Today was a day of excitement, Pastor preaching about "Go get Jesus!" Glory Hallelujah! In times of trouble, go get Jesus. The Word today was fire, coming straight from John chapter 11:1-44. Miracles happening left and right. I'm thankful the Lord still answers prayers, and being among the saints is pure joy. After the service, we had a feast and shared testimonies. Sister A's testimony gave me a better understanding of her journey with the Lord. We both have stories to tell, a testament to how far God has brought us.

I adore my Pastor and First Lady, finding solace at Emmanuel when I was hurting and in need of pruning. Relationships, church, family, job, friendships – they've all left scars. Without knowing who Jesus truly is, I might've lost my mind. There were times I wanted to die, but God refused to take my life. Even in a bad car accident on March 09, 2013, where I lost a finger, I survived, coming home the same day. God's amazing! I've been in the church for a while, playing the part without the Holy Ghost like I should've had. I had to repent for shacking up, lying, gossiping, and backbiting – keeping it real. I'm on the journey to deliverance. How about you?

Soul Searching

To hell with the devil, I'm not about gaining the whole world and losing my soul. There was this dude in my neighborhood once who had the audacity to say, "You're not a preacher." I shot back, "And you're not a drug dealer if you smoke what you're supposed to be selling." See, when it comes to Jesus Christ, I don't let anyone play games with me! I love people enough to hit them with the truth and respect them enough to believe they can handle it. It's high time for some self-love, self-respect, self-admiration, self-forgiveness, self-acceptance, self-nurturing – and guess what? Today is the grand kickoff!

Sure, they might have purposefully overlooked me, but God had bigger plans, purposefully catapulting me into His favor. I deserve to be treated right, and let me tell you, God's favor over my life beats any fancy resume. So, as I minister to myself with encouraging words, I'm reminded of God's directive to husbands: love your wife as God loves the church. And for us women, we were told to submit to our husbands. Well, Lord, here I am, a Woman of God, loving wholeheartedly. Even as I pen down this book, I've got love for someone, and my faith tells me God's got the power to save them. I won't stop praising God or praying for this individual. I know how to forgive and let go of grudges. The enemy's in the business of killing, stealing, and destroying, but Jesus? He came to give me life – and not just any life, but life more abundantly. Praise be to the good master!

Finding My Way

Praise the Lord's name! Hallelujah! I've come here to testify about my journey through relationships – three failed marriages, a few shack-ups, and a handful of boyfriends. There are times I feel like an absolute fool, but the Lord saw the need for me. Blessed assurance, Jesus is mine! I keep praying for Jesus to do something new in my life because, honestly, I need Him so badly. I tell myself, "You're a good woman, nothing's wrong with you," yet this loneliness persists. Jesus said He'll never leave or forsake me, so today, I declare He's here, even if I can't see it with my natural eyes – my spiritual eye sees it clearly. Stick with me, Lord, and I'll trust and never doubt you.

Teaching our children about love is so crucial. Growing up was tough – curse words, excessive drinking, and inappropriate things for young minds. I wanted out so bad that I married my first husband at twenty-one, in a tough marriage while pregnant. My son was born weighing only 4lbs with an opening down the middle of his head. Protecting him became my mission because of his tiny size.

My twin sister and I, despite not always seeing eye to eye, both suffered in relationships. We're good women, deserving of proper treatment. Mistreatment hurts, especially when it comes from someone you love deeply.

Having a moment, excuse me! Toxic people come and go, but with Christ, things get better. If it weren't for Jesus, life's unfairness might've crushed me. Frankie Thomas has been a blessing, providing a shoulder to cry on when needed, and I love her for being a great friend despite our unusual introduction. Today, I was a bit off, the enemy trying to provoke anger, but I kept my composure, remembering the Bible says, "be angry but do not sin."

All I want is a good, normal life and peace while serving the good master. Yet, stumbling blocks appear everywhere I turn. I just want to shout out to Jesus, my savior, master, teacher, and friend. My mind wandered back to February 15, 2013, when I was called to the Statesboro Jail. I thought it was about one of my sons, but it was me they were investigating. For a year, I went back and forth to court, and every time, Jesus was there. His command freed me – an encounter in a courtroom that echoed His presence. Even on my way to prison, God never left me alone. His power is unmatched.

Talking with my sisters about our childhood brings up
the question of family secrets. My father had both parents, but
there was still dysfunction. My mother, adopted by her aunt,
went through a different upbringing. Dark secrets linger in
families, mysteries that may never fully unravel.

Grandma's Hands

Oh, let me take you back to the days when I got
pregnant at sixteen. Grandma came to the house, and instead
of celebrating, she hoped I'd lose the baby. Yeah, that hit deep,
but hey, my son's now in his forties, and I've conquered a
mountain of challenges. Heaven and earth can do their thing,
but God's Word? That's unshakable. I started seeking God
more in my life, but back then, at sixteen, life was a bit of a
puzzle. I've always been a dreamer, thanks to my mom and
her numbers game. Dreams were a big deal back then, and
maybe still are.

So, God had His hands on me for a while. I believe I'm
called to prophecy, but to do that, I need to fully surrender to
God, keep my spirit clean, repent, forgive, and resist the
world's temptations. Tamela Mann's song "This Place"
became my anthem during the pain with Roo. I played it on
repeat, rebuking anything not of God in my spirit and home.

In the name of Jesus, I canceled Satan's assignments, taking charge over my family and declaring his power void.

God, being the MVP, answers my prayers on time. I pray for a clean heart and a right spirit, seeking guidance in fasting and prayer. Life's been a roller coaster lately, hurting so bad that God became my refuge. It's crazy how the ones you love, and help can hurt you the most. All I did was pray for sanity, fearing the devil was playing with my mind. Writing this book became my therapy, bringing my heart and mind back on track. I was way behind on the call God had on my life – had to make my call and election sure.

Negative vibes around you? That's a recipe for a bad spirit. I don't stick around those who don't lift me up. Tensions from others affect my atmosphere, and I can't be having that. Had a chat with Roosevelt recently, asked him why the disrespect and talking down, especially in front of a white lady. Maybe that's his idea of feeling big. No woman should want to witness another woman hurting, right? When a man treats you like his lady, you've got every right to feel special. It's a vibe, and it should be uplifting, not the other way around.

Resilient Roots

As I spilled the beans earlier in my book, I've been through it all – spat on, jaw broken, pushed down, punched in the face, and called names that would make a sailor blush. Feeling like a wounded soldier returning from war. Now, let me tell you about Roosevelt. At one point, he was the bee's knees, a real gem. I'm still trying to decode what went wrong. One thing's for sure, he wasn't ready to ditch the streets. This guy was mean, especially with his words. He even paraded a white woman out of the room, as if to say, "Look at what he's got." Classy, right?

For three whole years, he used me like a worn-out rug. No love, no genuine interest. How do I know? Well, every time he swung by it was the same broken record about being broke. No dates, no quality time – nada. God peeled back the layers, but I, in my love-blinded state, brushed it all off, thinking he loved me. Turns out, he didn't. Crystal clear now, ain't it?

Chapter 7: Growing Beyond the Pain

As I pour my heart into this book, I'm typing through tears and more tears. It's easy for others to say, "Don't do this, don't do that," but when you're the one bleeding on the inside with no one to stanch the flow, it's a different story. Can you believe at 53, I'm still grappling with this hurt? Sometimes it feels like life is squeezing the breath out of me.

When does the pain subside? When does it finally pack its bags and leave? Jesus is the only place I've found solace. My buddies at Woman in Transition and Help Group, especially Chaplin Jones, have been my lifeline. She's always like, "Carolyn, you know the answer, want me to spell it out?" And I'm there nodding, "Yes!"

Today was church, and even though you try not to show it, sometimes the pastor's words feel tailor-made for you. The pulpit hits your heart, and you're sitting there saying "Amen," all while trying not to let on how hard the Word is hitting home. Mercy, oh Lord! I felt like I was bleeding right there on the church floor. But you know what? God's got His first aid kit ready for me.

Our church family is something special. Sure, we have our squabbles, but love smoothens out the wrinkles. Prayer and communion with the Lord make everything feel right. I don't want to fake a holy life—I want to be a pillar of truth. I need Jesus every day, not just on occasion. I've come to realize I can't navigate life without the Lord.

Today, my mind wandered down the road of self-pity. I found myself crying while driving down the highway. No one in the car but me. Growing up, I often felt like no one cared. I had to step away from the computer because some memories cut too deep. Sometimes, I have to keep moving so the enemy's darts miss their mark.

Brushstrokes of Redemption

Today, I had to have a heart-to-heart with God, and the message I brought to the divine table was, "It is well." Drawing inspiration from 2 Kings Chapter 4:8, sometimes you just have to declare to a situation that it's well. People can be spirit murderers, you know? Men and women get entangled for all sorts of reasons, and it's disheartening that this mess has been around since Bible days. I've whispered to the Lord in private, asking where I might have gone astray so that He could reward me openly. The burning question now is, are there any good men left? Can a good man find a good woman in me? Because believe it or not, I feel and think I am a good woman.

My father raised a good one, after all. Maybe we should get marriage insurance just in case things go south. Where does that leave either spouse if it doesn't work out? Beats me! I've been down some really rocky relationship roads, and the last one with Roosevelt was a wild ride. He was a 60-year-old player and street-smart guy. Thought he was a good man until all his not-so-great habits came out of hiding. Did a 180 and started acting like a kid. Frankie, a good friend, watched as he wanted me to go through his aunt for everything, treating him like a child when he was a 60-year-old man. But it's all good now; God's got my back and knows every twist and turn I've been through.

Why treat me like garbage? Lord, make me over, that's my prayer. It's been a journey, a tough one, but I'm on the road to recovery. Lord, take the wheel of this crazy life and steer me higher. I've learned my lesson – nothing and no one comes before God. I once wanted someone who didn't want me, but God wanted me. I've witnessed countless women go through the painful cycle of love's betrayal. I know men get hurt too, but the ones I've dated have left me with wounds that run deep. I've asked the Lord, "Why do these men disrespect me?"

In all things shewing thyself a pattern of good works: in doctrine shewing uncorrupted, gravity, sincerity, Sound speech, that cannot be condemned; that he that is of the contrary part may be ashamed, having no evil thing to say of you. Titus 2:7-8

Unveiling Resilience Within

"I've been singing God's praises all day, feeling genuinely good about who I am. My truth doesn't scare me anymore, and I won't cut out pieces of myself to make others comfortable.

Today, when I stepped into the bank, the teller and I started praising God together, keeping our focus on Jesus. She shared a valuable piece of advice – always keep your eyes on God. The Word of God holds true, and I'm living by Isaiah 54:4: 'Fear not; for thou shalt not be ashamed, neither be thou confounded; for thou shalt not be put to shame: for thou shalt forget the shame of thy youth, and shalt not remember the reproach of thy widowhood anymore.'

Lord, guide me on the right path. I've endured so much pain that sometimes I question why I'm still here. I've loved deeply and wasted precious time on men who didn't deserve me. Looking back hurts, so I try not to dwell on those painful times with anyone. I prioritize myself and the Lord above all, finding peace in that. As I reflect on my past, I've taken a lot of punches, but now I live for God and die for God. Holy Ghost, help me! There are more books within me, and I know I have to release all these pains. I've helped everyone, and I don't regret it, but why was I treated so poorly?

Today, I reached out to Litia, one of the young ladies in my group, guided by the Holy Spirit. We never truly know what each other is going through, so we shared our feelings about life's challenges. Litia has been through a lot, and as we fellowshipped, I asked her to stay connected. Sometimes, I need someone to talk to and share my feelings.

Nobody truly understands your pain but you. Getting this book out was crucial. I love my father, but us girls suffered a great deal. All three of my sisters are married, but here I am. To find happiness: let go of what's gone, be grateful for what remains, and look forward to what is coming."

Broken Beginnings

"I've got four amazing sons, each with different fathers, but I always made sure to pave the way for them. Sadly, they never witnessed anyone I dated or married treating me like a lady. This, I think, messed me up mentally and physically, affecting both me and my sons. Sometimes, I get a negative response that makes me feel they don't respect me as their mother, and that really hurts. My oldest son is distant, not calling or coming around. The second oldest doesn't communicate much, despite us living in the same city. The only two I hear from are my youngest ones. Every day, I pray for a better relationship with all my children. I am incredibly proud of what and who they have become. Every day, I strive to see them prosper. My life has been a rollercoaster, but I made it this far, and I know I can keep going.

I want to thank everyone who looked down on me and thought I wouldn't be anything. Blessings to all my users and abusers. Thank God for my church family and friends who had no idea where I came from—a young black female from the woods of Highway 17, living in a single-wide trailer with four sisters, my mother, and father. God, I am so thankful. The Lord has made a way for me countless times. I faced so much abuse, not just in relationships but within my own family. I had only one aunt on my father's side who loved and stood up for me. Everyone else seemed to harbor hatred. My mother's older sister, who is now deceased, told a lie about me before she died, and there was no way for me to prove otherwise. What do you do? Pray and ask God to heal your hurts.

My own family took me to court and sued me. That hit me like a brick. No matter what anyone else said, I could never have taken her to court. That hurt me to the core. It felt like mistreatment and hatred surrounded me everywhere I turned. Writing this book has brought me closer to God and helped me forgive others by putting it all on paper.

The most painful thing is losing yourself in the process of loving someone too much, forgetting that you are special too. - Ernest Hemingway. I believe I forgot how important I was, always trying to please others."

Chapter 8: Whispers of Abandonment

"On September 2, 2022, I had a really disturbing conversation with Roo. Talking to him is always a challenge; it's like he never knows how to hold a decent conversation, especially with me. Feeling down, I decided to call my son Javis. I was sad, and I started by saying, 'Javis, I am your mother, and when you all talk to me nasty in front of your wives and others, it hurts me.' I realized I needed to have a similar conversation with my other boys. It seemed like everyone in my family, relationships, and friendships treated me as if I were some naive women, and I couldn't stand it.

Heading to work feeling terrible, I remembered what my friend told me. She advised me to call Ms. Yvonne, and when I did, I discovered she was going through a breakup too. Despite her situation, she seemed in much better shape than I was. Recalling the events with Roosevelt, I began to cry. It became clear that Roosevelt didn't love me at all; he built me up just to tear me apart when he felt like it. Grateful for the amazing women in my life, their prayers and encouraging words mean everything. Taking a chance on this gentleman, Roosevelt, was a mistake.

When I talk about how he treats me, all I hear is that he treats other women the same way. No woman should be disrespected, regardless of color. I needed this time to myself. I'm not involved romantically or physically, but these bad relationships make me fear getting involved with a man again. I trust God in everything, but I definitely need help – healing, evaluating, learning, and progressing.

Roosevelt almost tore the heart out of me, showing no remorse for the pain he caused. Jersey never apologized either; he insisted I caused all the problems. Most of the time, he'd say, 'Carol, nobody likes you.' That hurt, coming from someone who was supposed to love me. God, help me! I was a good lady, and men could sense it from a mile away. I would never have hurt either one of them. During my time with Jersey, he never loved me; it was a convenience. He even told me he would stay in the other room while I dated and saw Roosevelt. Roosevelt was unpredictable, and I was shocked when he showed up knocking on my window this morning, claiming he wanted to see if I had the title for his car, even though he knew I didn't have it."

My intuition assured me that he came by for other reasons. I decided on Sunday not to call or text this man and deleted all his numbers out of my phone. People want what they want when they want it. Understanding his relationship with his aunt, rather he does good or bad she's gonna love him. Me, I did so much for the ungrateful. Roosevelt never treated me with respect, he turned into a real live devil. He sent anger, hurt, and rejection, told me to give my love to someone else he did not want it. I caught you with a Caucasian woman and you protect her and not me. How could I forget such an unlawful act? He just did not care about me at all. Yes! I hurt like a hole was in my heart and nobody I told about this understood how I felt, not even Frankie because she was my friend and his Auntie.

Embracing Solitude

I can vividly recall Charles, Biscuit, LC, and E – the worst of the worst. These men entered my life after Charles, my ex-husband. I left behind what I thought were all my troubles to embark on a new life in Atlanta, only to encounter men who were even worse than the country men I had left behind. I remember dating a guy named Dee; he was so nasty and disrespectful. I met him at my job, where he worked as a forklift driver. One day, running late to pick him up after an early finish due to a meeting, he became furious. Upon my arrival, he grabbed me around my neck and started choking me. After that day, I wanted nothing to do with him. Who in hell gets mad at someone about their own car? I'd call myself stupid, but in reality, I was just a kind-hearted woman that men like him weren't used to. I am very stable, but all this mistreatment could have caused a serious breakdown if not for God! Many nights, I would lie in bed and just cry, especially after the breakup with Roosevelt. He claimed he wanted me to advance in my ministry, which I did, but the real reason for the breakup was the Caucasian female.

I respect myself and deserve better than what was being offered. Ladies, any time a man is seeing you but insists you're not his woman, believe him. No man will ever be with me for sexual pleasure unless he is my husband. Of course, they may miss you, but caring about your hurt? I don't think so.

Deciding to seek therapy has been immensely helpful, especially when I couldn't talk to my family or best friend about my feelings. People often fail to understand what you're going through, so why waste time trying to explain? I used to share with my twin, but she didn't understand me. Of course, I'd turn to my sister next to us, and she'd tell you exactly how she felt about a matter.

Every family has its share of problems, but the foundation is love. My emotions always run deep; my heart is genuinely loving and kind. I try to treat everyone with respect, even if I may not fully grasp their intentions. I felt an urgent need to express what was simmering within me. Family members seemed to anticipate my struggles, not visible on the outside but marked by internal battles. Coping with these challenges is a process I'm currently navigating by the grace of Almighty God. Instead of dwelling on the pain caused by those who hurt me, I questioned, "Why, Lord?" Yet, there's a realization that they have moved on with their lives. My primary longing has always been for a genuine love relationship, something I have yet to encounter.

As mentioned earlier, I opted for counseling, especially given the profound hurt caused by Roosevelt. During our discussions, my counselor dropped a truth bomb: "If nothing changes, nothing changes." This resonated deeply – a call for self-care and a return to selflessness, as Roo had become a selfish man. I needed to find myself amidst the chaos. What motivates someone to treat you poorly? I hope that those who caused me pain read my book and comprehend the depth of the hurt they inflicted. I've learned not to let anybody make me lose myself or my sanity. Trusting in God, I refrain from questioning why these things happened to me. It's just okay now; there was a deeper version of me inside waiting to emerge. It feels liberating not to worry about a man in my house without the sweet aroma of love in the air.

Roosevelt's actions were incomprehensible to me; all he seemed to care about was his own desires, seeking them in the late-night streets. At sixty, he embodied a devilish spirit. One day, divine justice will unfold; it's okay to let them treat you however they want because karma is real. Where I come from, men respect their women, and no other woman would dare disrespect his lady. Today, men casually claim women as "just friends," suggesting a multitude of female friends, which is unsatisfactory. Men of this kind can go live with their mothers for the rest of their lives. Roosevelt labeled me insecure and childish, but every concern I voiced was a reality he lived.

Reclaiming My Voice

When a woman senses something deep in her gut, and that feeling never wavers, she knows she's right on the mark. Don't treat me like an object and expect me to turn a blind eye. He wanted the freedom to see me whenever he pleased and be with others, all while informing me of it—that's pimping. The audacity! And mind you, he was fifty-nine and not exactly in stellar shape. Why would I let anyone, him or whoever else, make me feel any less of a woman?

Honestly, I suspect something happened in this man's childhood to lead him to behave in such an unsatisfactory manner. His track record of leaving his first wife, a beautiful woman, with two small children in Miami, suggests a pattern of abandoning women for others. Sometimes, we end up loving the wrong people, and that's where the trouble begins. Patience is a virtue, and good things supposedly come to those who wait, but for some, no amount of waiting leads to change. The devil, you see, doesn't hide all the time; he occasionally lets you know exactly where he stands.

Jersey, in his moments of honesty, used to say, "I told you I was the devil's advocate; you should have listened." He hit the nail on the head. In reality, there wasn't much disparity between the two men; their behaviors were strikingly similar. Both gifted me tears and a shattered heart. I came to Atlanta seeking a fresh start, making progress until I crossed paths with Jersey. His accent and those melancholy eyes captivated me. I believed he was a good man in need of love, especially from a good woman.

He once remarked, "I like how you look out for me," and that marked the beginning of what I thought would be a great relationship. However, he eventually returned to Atlanta to stay with me permanently, and he brought along two nieces, her husband, and a baby. All of us cramped into a one-bedroom apartment. The nieces, unfortunately, turned out to be disrespectful and nasty to me in my own home. Wrong decision, indeed.

They would sneak into the bathroom, shut the door, and chatter about me, all while I lay in bed right by the door. Looking back, I recall allowing things that should never have happened. Despite working two jobs, I was the sole contributor to the household. Jersey eventually landed a job paying twenty-five dollars an hour. I remember his niece urging him to keep using the unpleasant term for me. We exchanged silent glances, no words spoken. It's alright, though; I made it through all of that to declare this – I love myself enough to keep moving forward.

And forward I went, leading me to Roo. He worked downtown where I was employed, and I used to observe him, trying to grasp this man. With a great personality and a physique like a muscle man, he took his job seriously and didn't pay attention to women. Yet, during breaks, we'd talk and laugh together. Even after I stopped working there, I'd go down just to see him. He'd always kiss me on my forehead and give me a hug. I sensed that we'd eventually get together, and we did. He called to inform me he would be released in December 2018. At first, fear overwhelmed me, causing me to ignore his calls. So, he left a message.

"I'm coming home now, and you want to answer my calls." Feeling guilty, I picked up the phone. Big mistake! Now, I wish I had never invested my heart, mind, or soul into this toxic relationship. This man got out of prison and didn't follow through on anything he promised. Not seeing his kids, not looking for his supposedly deceased mother (dead to him, I guess). Signs were pointing me to leave, but I was in love with him. I genuinely believed he used and abused me, and I was exhausted and angry. I didn't want to be that person, so I started praying and seeking God on every level of faith. I've witnessed God's incredible work in my life. Listening to my testimony and others, I realize how awesome God is in His actions.

Chapter 9: Against the Odds

I found myself falling so far behind in completing my book, tangled in workplace turmoil with a 69-year-old woman whom I thought was a friend but turned out not to be. Amidst my struggles, Roo and I were facing health issues, and my finances were in shambles. It's funny how people assume you're doing better than them when, in reality, you're not. This older woman took me by surprise. It seemed like she was actively trying to get me fired. I decided to respond with silence, and even that bothered her. If we don't get along, why force a conversation?

So, I plead the blood of Jesus, trusting God to set things right. Engaging in some self-pampering, I am determined to rise above all I'm going through. I needed God to show up, and He did! You needed a miracle, and He knew it. Today, I'm praising God for His profound love, thanking Him for meeting my needs so completely, and celebrating His unwavering faithfulness. The Lord shows his true love every day. Psalm 42:8

If you believe in a God who controls the big things, you have to believe in a God who controls the little things. It is we, of course, to whom things look "little" or "big". Elisabeth Elliot I know God gives us daily benefits 68:19 That includes his kindness, his goodness, and his provision. The benefits besides being our practical daily needs, is ultimately God himself. He knows no limits.

I've prayed earnestly for God to bring peace into my life, sharing all my hurts and vulnerabilities. Ironically, my sisters, who keep tabs on my Facebook page, secretly get together and label me as crazy. Is it crazy to desire love? Is it crazy to wish for someone who genuinely cares about you? Maybe it seems that way to them, given their seemingly perfect marriages.

Despite the hurts inflicted by those close to me, I continue to pray for them and harbor love in my heart. As I mentioned earlier in my book, every person who entered my life post-divorce proved to be challenging. Coming from a small town in Screven County, where everyone knew each other, and being associated with my husband's well-known family in the church world, my ex-husband, deemed an Elder, unwittingly became an instrument to undermine my anointing. In the face of disrespect, all-night escapades, and financial neglect, I remained committed to a marriage that was tearing me apart. I've worked tirelessly throughout my life, currently holding two jobs, driven by the love I have for my grandchildren—seven in total, comprising two girls and five boys. They are my legacy.

Throughout my life, in moments of heartbreaks and breakthroughs, I've longed to speak sincerely from my heart. We are cautioned not to be ignorant of the devil's tactics, and in my case, he came through family, friends, and those I believed loved and cared for me—mostly men.

Defying Despair

I recently had a falling out with my two sisters, and it felt like the devil was stirring up trouble. Amidst their anger, hurtful words were exchanged, and one sister even threatened to break my jaw. She accused me of being crazy and insisted I should tell my son that I used his child support to take care of other men. It's worth noting that we didn't raise our children together; she was overseas with her family. Our conversations became circular, filled with hostility, and our relationship hit a breaking point. My twin sister, who often appears as the 'better twin' due to my outspoken and clownish nature, created distance, and currently, there's no communication between us.

During this challenging time, I was dealing with workplace issues, health problems, and financial strain, and only God truly understood the ache in my heart. Nights were spent alone, tearful, and sleepless, relying solely on prayer. I wondered when God would intervene, holding onto the belief that joy would come in the morning.

Desiring love and attention, all I seemed to encounter was rejection. Thanksgiving was spent working, but my dear friend Frankie Thomas made dinner for me. Surprising her afterward, she was moved to tears, and we shared a heartfelt moment. Her family has been a source of support, and I trust that whatever God has in store will work for my good. As December approached, my excitement for Christmas grew. I cherish the opportunity to make my daughter-in-law feel special, craving the closeness of having a daughter.

Christmas was a joyous occasion spent with my daughter-in-law Reshea, my son Joshua Lee, six of my seven grandchildren, and two sons. However, as February arrived, I found myself pondering why my two oldest sons seem distant, suspecting external family interference. But my God keeps lifting my spirit. He's a way maker, a miracle worker.

This book chronicling my life has offered me profound insights, prompting me to reevaluate my priorities. I've lost the desire to engage with negativity. This year is about loving myself!

Roosevelt has been the love of my life, and I once questioned God about not having him yet. Surprisingly, God responded, stating it was because I gave Roosevelt my whole heart instead of Him. In a moment of repentance and seeking forgiveness, I acknowledged God's jealousy and confessed my misplaced focus. Despite the coldness and resentment from Roosevelt, causing me immense hurt, I realized I was a wounded woman. Love had become a source of pain instead of joy, as my routine consisted only of going to church, working, and returning home. Depression crept in, requiring immediate prayer. Even as an Evangelist, I was still human, grappling with the power Roosevelt had over me due to my genuine love for him.

Recognizing that God specializes, I felt a divine intervention. I understand that love can be painful, and people only treat you as you allow. Despite my fear, I am determined to make it with God's help. It's crucial not to get so entangled in others that we forget the love of God. I'm committed to manifesting everything I've set out to achieve. I've become my own support system, applauding my own victories. As I reflect on the past, the instances of physical and verbal abuse from Roosevelt, catching him with another woman, and the subsequent humiliation, I realize the depth of hurt. Despite my commitment to family and the belief that blood is thicker than water, I grapple with the unfathomable pain of being mistreated after doing everything possible for someone. At this point, I'm not interested in helping or loving another man unless God explicitly guides me in that direction.

Endurance

The Bible beautifully says that a man washes a woman with the water of the Word, reminding her of her identity in Christ (Ephesians 5:26). It's perplexing how some sons, despite professing love, mistreat their mothers and others. I've raised four sons, instilling in them the values of love and respect for all women.

Reflecting on my own life, profound love seemed elusive. The yearning for love led me to feel unloved and uncared for, though my children know of my love through both actions and words. I've always tried hard to earn love, but it resulted in being used and unappreciated by the men I loved. Rejection, resentment, abuse – that's what I received in return. I prayed for God to break every chain and destroy the devil's attempts to ruin my life. Preaching became my passion, a way to let God use me.

Waking up today, I glanced at my past, realizing that nobody seemed to want me – no baby daddy, no husband, no boyfriend, no family member. I felt like a nobody, facing criticism and mistreatment. But God! The pain persists at times, and tears flow as I pen down these words.

A songwriter once wrote, "It's not right, but it's okay." Like Oprah in "The Color Purple," my life has been a constant fight. This morning, the tears flow, and I implore God to take away the pain. My life has been dented in many areas, but I plead the blood of Jesus against the enemy. I long for peace in my life, my children's lives, and my grandchildren's lives. I express gratitude for my daughter-in-law Reshea Lee, with whom I've bonded deeply. Despite challenges with my other daughter-in-law and son due to family hearsay, I still love them and pray for healing. I haven't met my grandson yet, but he resembles me. What more can I do, Lord? In the midst of bruised love, I turn to the Lord, waiting for His guidance. Hallelujah!

Chapter 10: Silent Echoes

How do you move on when thoughts keep resurfacing? I can't shake off the last hurtful words Roosevelt said to me, "she got more than you, I promise you that!" Why a man would say that to any woman baffles me. I went out of my way to help him, even sacrificing for those who'd later betray me. I now understand why women, once they're over someone, never look back—sometimes a person's presence becomes sickening.

Roosevelt had a love for money, willing to use anyone to get it, making questionable decisions. I'm still seeking God for my own healing, grappling with various challenges. But I'm emerging stronger, thanks to God's grace. My prayers extend to my family, including my sisters, nieces, nephews, and mother. I cherish my family and want God to use me for His glory, hoping this book resonates with women facing similar hardships.

Shoutout to my good friend John Hughes, who patiently listened even when tired of my complaints. God bless his niece, "Prophetess Fireball," a true blessing. Gratitude to all who touched my life, including the First Lady and Evangelist S.F. I've learned significant life lessons: give, but don't allow yourself to be used; love, but don't let your heart be abused; trust, but don't be naive; listen, but don't lose your own voice. Time lessens the miss, and crossing certain lines can quickly change everything. Now, I'm watering myself, realizing I can't partner with the enemy and expect manifestations from God. Everyone leaves eventually, either by choice or force.

Learning to live without Roosevelt, I still miss him at times. Yet, I won't betray anyone who ensured I was okay when no one else did. I let go of what let go of me, striving for happiness amidst my challenges. I've discovered I can do all things through Christ. Missing someone doesn't negate the understanding that you're better off without them. It's about honesty and awareness—nobody is always right, and abusers demand to be seen positively.

I've felt low three times, cursed out by black men I loved, subjected to unnecessary names. The mistreatment from my own race, while others watch, raises a profound question about the state of the black community. I've chosen to live alone, not complaining, and resisting the attempts of those who tried to bury me. I now realize I'm a seed.

It's time to forget those who forgot me, not allowing pain to break me. You can discern what the enemy fears by recognizing what he attacks. As I conclude my book, the enemy tries to throw rocks, but because Jesus lives, I can face tomorrow. I'm thankful for those who loved me despite my flaws. Writing this has been a journey, and as I look back, I want to inspire and touch someone's life. I've learned the hard way about love, and I'm committed to passing on these lessons to my sons.

I desire a lot from life, and I want to have touched and inspired someone. This last relationship took a toll, forcing me to set my priorities straight. I've never shared my feelings on paper for others to read, but I believe it's time to inspire others with my story. I never had a man stand before a woman and declare that she has more than me. It was a revelation about his character. I've been loyal to someone who wasn't my husband, maybe not even a boyfriend. God clearly states not to be unequally yoked with unbelievers, and I looked over the signs. My sons often remind me that I have them and don't need anyone else, but they have their own lives and families.

Rediscovering Myself

I am a beautiful, loving, and kind woman, always ready to lend a helping hand. Despite enduring years of abuse, I was sharing with my friend's husband that if I had all the money and credit, I used to assist others, I'd be a wealthy woman here in Atlanta, living alone in an apartment and taking care of all my needs. God is truly good and worthy of all praise. He knew me before I was even formed, so all these experiences had to unfold. People in the church, in my family, on my job, and within my circle treated me less than I deserved, but through it all, I kept praying and trusting God for everything. Like an eagle, I will soar, and soon everyone who doubted my potential will see what God has in store for me next. The Lord is good to all, and His tender mercies are evident in His works, and I am one of His works.

I carry a positive women's ministry within me, often reflecting on Queen Vashti from the book of Esther, a brave woman who risked her life by standing up for her convictions and saying no to the king's inappropriate request. She knew her worth, and we, as women, should demand respect and honor in our rightful place. Some might disagree, but I recall a Caucasian woman declaring that she had more than me when I stood before her. The last man I dated echoed these words. In that moment, the clarity regarding his intentions was undeniable. Today, I stand tall, proclaiming victory over every man who thought I wasn't good enough, who cheated, lied, used, and trampled on my heart. With Christ as my head, I made it through suffering, depression, and heartache. Even my own children didn't always respect me, but I was there, offering help, giving my money, love, and kindness.

If you have nothing to offer, people tend to overlook you. My name has been dragged through the mud, but I'll never forget my mother's advice to pray for those who've wronged me. At seventy-six years young, my mother's wisdom resonates deeply with me. I love her more now because I comprehend the challenges she faced as a married woman. This is my life story, my journey laid bare in this book. I've reached a turning point, observing everything through the spirit of Christ; I can't afford to live without Him. He is everything to me, offering eternal life, and I've accepted His call. My entire being belongs to God; I owe no one anything but the Lord. He has blessed me with sisters, friends, aunts, uncles, cousins, grandchildren, and children. I never expected these people to betray me; I believed in the power of love. Don't get me wrong—I haven't always been saved, and I've fallen short in my life.

I can't speak on behalf of others, but I can speak for myself. Despite my struggles every day, I still love these people. God's benefits sustain me daily—Amen to that! My hope and prayer are that one day, the Williams family can come together and genuinely love one another. Typically, our family gatherings are marked by funerals, the last one being for my sweet Aunt Liz. She treated every relative as if she were our grandmother, Ollie Mays Williams. My father, grandmother, and Aunt Liz are all gone now.

Families often harbor untold secrets, lies, hate, and revenge. I've taken on the role of preaching and teaching. I'm not the Carolyn you may have heard negative things about;

take the time to get to know me for yourself. Yes, I might have been something else in the past, but today, I am a new creature in Christ. I have a thirteen-year-old great niece who, having overheard countless conversations about me from grown folks, often questions what she thought I was. I always tell her, "I am what God says I am, nothing more, nothing less." The younger generation is different from what we were in our time, and I pray especially for those children who can't help themselves. As the hymn goes, "Little ones to Him belong, they are weak, but He is strong!"

Threads of Hope

Lord, you've done it for me so many times, making a way when it seemed impossible. I'm sharing my story straight from the heart. Even at work, dealing with haters who don't know me, only what they've heard. So, I'm setting the record straight and telling my own story! Throughout my life, I felt like I was constantly being stepped on, facing more trials and tribulations than I can count. I loved fiercely, but it often felt unreciprocated.

Frankie Thomas and my friend Josie, God rest her soul, were inspirations in my life. I don't throw around the term "friend" lightly; too many people are just looking to use someone for their own gain.

Where were they when I was sick, struggling to pay bills, stuck in jail, or in desperate need? I recall paying an attorney to represent me, and on the day of court, he dropped my case, kept my money, and claimed to be a man of God. When I asked for a refund, he refused. But God lifted up a standard, and I stand today with a table set in the presence of my enemies. Hallelujah! They said I wouldn't make it, that I wouldn't amount to anything. Well, I'm on my way, and I feel like preaching right now. Oh, how I love Jesus! Help me, Holy Ghost!

This isn't just my book; it's God's book. I'm merely preaching His gospel according to the Bible, and it marks the turning point of my life. Thank you, Roosevelt, the last man who used and looked down on me. All I wanted was love, but when the good Lord stepped in, He became all the love I needed. I may have looked like shattered glass, but I'm a beautiful piece of artwork. I am the CEO of Carolyn, and I thank the women in transition, Yvonne, Anika, Eloise, Pastor Nelson, Ruby, Wanda, and many more who went above and beyond for me. I recognize your patience.

God has something lined up for me, and I'm more than ready to move forward. I dream, have visions, and talk to God daily. He's in control. Love yourself, adore yourself. No longer do I sit around wondering why nobody wants me or what's wrong with me. Baby, something's wrong with the people who mistreat you. They'll have to come back and apologize one day. Praise is what I do in the middle of every storm. Worship until you pass out. Keep praising Him. I want women to know that greater is He that is in you than he that is in the world. My God is awesome, and all things are possible with God.

Chapter 11: From Darkness to Dawn

Many times, in my life, I've endured pain—days, weeks, months, and years. Through laughter and tears, I made it. I've been part of ministries where people tried to suppress my anointing, witnessing God using me while others attempted to sabotage my path. Testing spirits by the spirit, discerning the truth beyond what eyes could see, navigating through church politics and cliques that I despise. We are all designed for a purpose, and relationships of any kind should hold value.

I am a mother, yet for two and a half years, I didn't see any of my children. My second oldest was incarcerated, unable to visit, and the others, though they wrote letters, never came, or sent money. In Atlanta's TC program, I worked hard, saved, got an apartment, and refused to return to my old ways. The system is corrupt, and as a first-time offender, I thank God for that part of my life. Walking by faith, not sight, is not always what people want to hear, but it is my truth. I take time for my baby sister, understanding the loneliness I once felt. My passion for reading and writing, especially poetry, helped me express the love I have for God, the one I depend on in all circumstances.

Frankie, I love for standing by me, and I've faced hurts, but I don't ask why anymore. Be still and know that He is God.

I've given so much of myself that it drained me. I lift my head now; nobody will make me feel less than the woman I am. I still believe in love, but only with the right person sent by God. I pray for my ex-husbands, ex-boyfriends, family, and friends. I've survived, scars remain, but the wounds are healed.

Throughout my life, I fought for space in people's lives, often being overlooked. But God never looked over me. Money brought temporary love, and I've been picked at on my job and accused unjustly. God is the author of my life, and with Him, I can make it. Jealousy surrounds me, and I've been overlooked in church, work, and family. Repenting daily, I challenge many things.

Reflecting on past hurts, like finding my ex-husband at my so-called best friend's house, I choose not to gamble with my life anymore. The devil uses anything close to destroy, but God bears my burdens. I've had hard times, helping many who wouldn't reciprocate. Hated without cause, even by those close to me. In 2023, I aim to finish strong, battling with some things but holding on to God's unchanging hand.

God's Love

My redeemer lives, assuring me of a better tomorrow. Just like a butterfly in transition, I am undergoing beautiful and colorful transformations. No longer concerned about who likes or loves me because I've found love within myself. I navigate through work, where friendships dictate certain positions, and live in a space away from the crowd. Even in church, where respect may lack, I find solace in the fact that God sees and knows.

God, sitting high and looking low, answers prayers when we reach out to Him. He sends people into our lives to guide us to the next step. Like an infant learning to walk, we must keep trying and pushing forward. I take pride in my resilience, enduring internal struggles that could have broken me, yet my heavenly father sustained me. I acknowledge that I'm not the only hurting woman; however, pouring my emotions onto paper helps me breathe and exhale.

Reflecting on past hurts inflicted by friends, lovers, family, and even my own blood, I remember moments of immense pain. My strength today is a testament to the love and sacrifices made by my father when he ran up a hill to reach me during a car accident. I've helped many, but when I needed assistance, they weren't there for me.

Grateful for working with Pastor Nelson, who strives to share God's message, I pray for the deliverance of my family from generational curses. I believe in the power of God to heal, deliver, and set free. I've encountered high dignitaries in churches, witnessing their failure to bring true transformation. Bishop Jones's teachings resonate we are not lords over God's people, and we must be mindful of our behavior in God's house.

Coming with a purpose, there was a time when confusion clouded my thoughts, but realigning myself with the Lord helped me move forward. I acknowledge my dependence on God, more essential than food, water, or clothing. I rebuke the enemy's attempt to destroy my family, staying close to God, who gave His life for mine. Despite external perceptions, I know I'm created for greatness by the one and only, Jesus. Writing helps release the bottled-up emotions that held me back.

Primarily, my aim is to share stories about the complexities of various relationships that often obstruct our paths. I used to be someone who loved intensely, but over time, I transformed into a person reluctant to love at all. Recognizing that each person is unique, I delved into understanding why I found myself trapped in repetitive cycles. The introspection led me to a crucial realization—I yearned for someone to care about me the way I cared for and loved others. However, it seemed that no one reciprocated unless I was providing financial support.

In a poignant moment, I recollect the wise words of my late Aunt Liz, who advised me to cease helping those who didn't reciprocate. I reminisce about her unwavering support, and a pang of regret surfaces as I recall a time when she needed financial assistance for medication, and I couldn't reciprocate. Bless her soul, for she was a fantastic and caring aunt to me. As I sit here writing, tears well up in my eyes, flowing from the depth of my heart. Oh, God, I am heavy-hearted this morning; Jesus, help me through this emotional weight.

Chapter 12: A Journey of Reclamation

In the tapestry of life, my narrative has woven through the intricate threads of relationships, revealing the complexities that often obstruct our journey. Once a fervent lover, time sculpted me into a person hesitant to embrace love. Amidst the diverse tapestry of individuals, I embarked on a journey of self-discovery, unraveling the enigma of my repetitive cycles. The introspection bore a vital truth—I craved reciprocal care, a love mirroring the depth of my own. Yet, it seemed elusive, materializing only when financial support was in the offering.

In a poignant reflection, the echoes of my late Aunt Liz's wisdom resound, urging me to disengage from one-sided relationships. I cherish the memory of her unwavering support, and a twinge of remorse surfaces when I recall a moment of inability to reciprocate her need for financial assistance. Bless her soul, for she was an extraordinary and nurturing aunt. As I pen these lines, tears blur my vision, drawn from the profound well of my heart. Oh, God, the weight on my heart is palpable this morning; Jesus, guide me through this emotional labyrinth.

And so, as I conclude this chapter of my life, I find solace in the lessons learned, the strength gained, and the resilience forged. May these words resonate with those who have walked similar paths, navigated the maze of relationships, and yearned for reciprocal love. In the end, it is the love we give, receive, and learn to extend to ourselves that shapes the true narrative of our lives. As this chapter closes, I step forward with hope, carrying the echoes of the past into a future where self-love triumphs overall.

About the Author

Carolyn Michelle Williams, Born in Augusta, GA July 13, 1968, to Robert Williams and Juanita Roberson Williams. A twin sister Janet Renee Williams, also born four minutes prior to her birth. She is the mother of four boys, Darrell C. Williams, Terrell M. Roberson, Javis M. Robbins, Joshua S. Lee. Carolyn is a licensed Evangelist, Member of Women in Transition Group, a Motivational Speaker, Member of Immanuel Church of God in Christ. A mother, sister, friend, aunt, cousin. She has had hills to climb, with the good Lord she has leaped into places she never thought she would go. God gets all the glory out of her story! May her readers know that you can make it through your storms. Because he (the Lord) lives I can face tomorrow. God Bless!

CAROLYN WILLIAMS

"Hold on, you can make it; hold on, everything will be alright," is the refrain to a song that Carolyn loves. I, too, love this song as its performed by Sounds of Blackness. Our love of music has strengthened the bonds of friendship that has formed between me and her. I had no idea how things would work out when she first came to provide her housekeeping services several months ago. I quickly came to realize that she was a professional with a strong work ethic. Because of her work ethic, we often take time to listen to music, mostly religious, together, and talk about a wide range of topics. Family and current events are usually the topic of most of our conversations.

Carolyn's strong religious beliefs frequently permeate her thoughts, and I have come to know that she is very active in her church. Someone once said, "To one who has faith, no explanation is necessary." This aptly applies to Carolyn as she demonstrates this through her words and deeds. Her pleasant demeanor and breadth of knowledge are behaviors that make her a strong woman. I am certain that her life story will be an inspiration to all who read her book, and some may be motivated to tell their own stories. Autobiography is an important part of historical reference. Congratulations to Carolyn on her work and for joining the literary community.

Marcellus C. Barksdale, Ph.D.
Professor Emeritus
Morehouse College
Atlanta, GA

TO MY SISTER

Carolyn has always strived for what she wanted. Her writing her first book is not a surprise to me. God laid it upon her heart, and she accomplished it. As children, we played in the yard, talked about marriage, children, husbands, and jobs. Life is real, and as Shirly Caesar says, "Life wasn't playing this time."

Love, your twin,

Janet Williams Duncan

THE MYSTERY OF LOVE

Love is a mystery that no one can solve. Love in life is painful if no one turns the knob. Touching the surface makes it simpler to believe. When two are crushed together, it is hard to breathe. Days after, we leave each other's arms with sorrow in our eyes. The next morning, I lay in bed as the sun begins to rise. I see your face so clearly as darkness goes away. Too bad it's just a mystery and it's just foreplay.

Carolyn Williams

1996

www.ingramcontent.com/pod-product-compliance
Lightning Source LLC
Chambersburg PA
CBHW071213120626
46546CB00006B/2534